ANGELS AMONG US,

EARTH ANGELS

IDA GREENE, Ph.D.

Angels Among Us, Earth Angels.
Copyright © May 7, 2006 by P. S. I. Publishers, 2910 Baily Ave. San Diego, CA 92105. All rights reserved. No part of this publication may be reproduced, distributed, transmitted, transcribed, stored in a retrieval system, or translated into any language without the express prior agreement and written permission of the publisher.

ISBN 1-881165-20-5

Dr. Ida Greene, RN, Marriage, Family, Child Counselor has established **Our Place Center Of Self-Esteem,** a non-profit organization that assists At-risk children, and families coping with issues of violence and abuse. A portion of the sale from each book is donated to **Our Place Center Of Self-Esteem.**

Dr. Ida Greene speaks and conducts seminars, on personal/professional growth topics. www.idagreene.com.

ATTENTION COLLEGES AND UNIVERSITIES, CORPORATIONS, AND PROFESSIONAL ORGANIZATIONS

Quantity discounts are available on bulk purchases of this book for educational training purposes, fund-raising, or gift-giving, contact:

P. S. I. Publishers,
2910 Baily Avenue
San Diego, CA 92105
(619) 262-9951

OTHER PUBLICATIONS BY DR. GREENE

Books
Light the Fire Within You
Self-Esteem The Essence of You
Are You Ready For Success?
Soft Power Skills, Women and Negotiation™,
How to Be A Success In Business
How To Improve Self-Esteem In The African American Child
How To Improve Self-Esteem In Any Child
Money, How to get It, How to Keep It
Say Goodbye to Your Smallness, Say Hello to Your Greatness
Anger Management Skills for Children
Anger Management Skills for Men
Anger Management Skills for Women
Stirring Up the African American Spirit.

CDs
Money, How to Get It, How to Keep It
Light The Fire Within You

Video Cassettes
Soft Power Negotiation Skill
Light The Fire Within You
Self-Esteem, The Essence of You

For information, please contact Dr. Ida Greene at:
2910 Baily Avenue
San Diego, CA 92105
619-262-9951
www.idagreene.com

Contents

Introduction v

Chapter 1 1
The Divine Plan

Chapter 2 15
Our Angelic Quest

Chapter 3 34
How to Connect With Your Guardian Angel

Chapter 4 54
Angels Among Us, Earth Angels

Bibliography 70

Introduction

ANGELS AMONG US, EARTH ANGELS

This book is dedicated to all the many people now deceased: Rosa B. Maull, Veora Brooks Conley, and Ella B. Argrow, who have served as an Earth Angel to me, when I lived in San Diego, CA with no members of my family. To the my mom and Aunt Mary Stanberry, on the other side, who whispered words of encouragement to me when I was depressed. Yet there were other persons like Beverly Mitchell of Lightning Source, who added her angelic touch to my life. To all the people who offered their help through "Our Place Center of Self-Esteem;" and all the Angels posing as unknown strangers who crossed my path on frequent occasions, I thank you. I was inspired to write this book after my cousin, whom I called mama Betty, died July 11, 2005. She took on the role of mother to me after my mom died in 1994. She asked to serve as my mother, because of my feelings of loneliness and abandonment. Even though, she lived in Los Angeles, she kept in touch with me on a monthly basis to see how I was doing. She acted as a mother to many people in LA, and I discovered at her funeral that all of us were made to feel that we were her favorite adopted child, even though she had five children of her own that she adored and had a special relationship with each one.

It was at her funeral, I realized, we had been in presence of an Angel. I now believe that we are all sent by God, and that we are on a mission to earn our "angelic wings" through our service to humanity. Therefore, no life is in vain, and no life is greater than another, except in our commitment to giving and service to God's other children.

Any casual observation of infants will show you that we came into this life, with a vibrancy and unbounding energy that is often difficult to believe. A young child will eat when he is hungry, sleep when tired, and play for more hours than most adults can believe, because of the natural flow of their universal energy. In later life, when we adults tend to become more negative and stressed, we begin to close our hearts and minds and fail to receive the gifts that God wants us to have. I am hoping this book will open your mind and heart to the workings of God, the Holy Spirit of God, and Angels and show you how your life can change for the better when you allow all of them into your body and your life. We have been given free will, so God, the Holy Spirit, Jesus or the Angels will not come into your body or life without your permission. You must invite them in.

I would to thank Rachel Alexander Carty (Chelah) and her friend for helping with the typing to enable me to take a sample of the book with me to *Book Expo America* in Washington DC, May 18–21, 2006. I was most humbled by receiving the "Self-Publisher of the Year" award in the African American Pavilion.

Ida Greene

Chapter 1
The Divine Plan

We all have the potential for GREATNESS, to allow Great things to occur through our lives; however we have to make it happen. Nothing happens on earth without our Divine intervention. What is the difference between Marilyn Monroe and Coretta Scott King? Coretta Scott King had a Divine and Great purpose for living and being on the planet that impacted the lives of women, men and children, we can not say the same about Marilyn Monroe. Every one of us is born to make a difference, to play our part, and transform our corner of the world. We may not become famous, but we can live lives of compassion, understanding, forgiveness, justice, speak out for truth., live with joy, gusto and gentleness. Why do so many of us settle for small problems, and small lives?

I think too many of us fail to grab hold of our personal power, our Divine Angelic selves. I am of the opinion that we are trying to find our way back home to: God, our Divine self, our Divinity. We have forgotten who we are. We are an expression of God, made in His image and likeness. God lives inside each of us, this song says it best.

It's In Every One of Us
It's (God) in every one of us,
To be wise, Find you heart,

Open up both your eyes.
We can all know everything,
Without ever knowing why,
It's in every one of us, By and by.
It's in every one of us, To be free,
Find your Self, Open your eyes and see.
We can all have everything
Without ever knowing how,
It's in every one of us, Here and now.
AUTHOR UNKNOWN

SEEING IS BELIEVING

If you want miracles to occur in your life, you must change your thoughts from Believing is Seeing to Seeing is Believing. When you can believe before you see the results, miracles will occur right before your eyes. One incident readily comes to mind. I had an Amway small business, whose name today is Quick Start, I loved the cleaning products then and still love and use them today. I wanted to hit the top producer level, of $7,500 volume for the month however I was $4,500.00 short of volume and had no way to reach that goal. However, I saw myself reaching the goal but I could not figure out how it was going to happen. When I went to bed that night, I told God that I had done all that I could possibly do and that I was leaving the rest to him. The next morning I got a phone call at 6 am from one of my down line distributors who said she did not understand it, but she had been awakened at 5 am and was told to make a purchase of $4,500.00 worth of products, and that was exactly what I needed to make the position of Direct Distributor. We have to believe (have faith) and take action before God steps in. Now I never doubt, if I come close to doubting, I pray for help with my unbelief. The mind needs to know, however the Divine Spirit inside us, acts on our belief of knowing without a doubt that our needs will be met. It is God's good pleasure to give you the desires of your heart.

Another lesson we need to learn is how to detach from our earthly possessions. On march 2, 2006, I was driving on a dark street; I hit an object in the streets, suddenly my car starting making a loud noise like a tractor. I drove for one block to a lighted area, parked the car, and waited to see if it would restart. The car restarted so I thought I could make it home. I got on the freeway and the car started losing pressure, so I parked the car and called the towing company, who towed it to my home and parked it. The car ignition never restarted again. I became very depressed because I really loved that 190 E, green Mercedes. I bought it new in 1993. I became aware that I was attached to my Mercedes. I had once said that I was not attached to anything. However, God showed me that I had become attached to my green Mercedes, and the goal for me and all human beings is to not be attached to anything in the earthly realm, since we will eventually have to leave all behind for our eternal connection with God and our great Homecoming. Earth is our training camp where we practice growing stronger in patience, peace, unconditional love, acceptance, justice, tolerance, fairness, appreciation, approval, security, encouragement, joy and eternal bliss. When I can be in an accident, have my car totaled, I am unhurt or shook up, I know there is a God and that I have Angels watching over and protecting me. Also I was able to pay the $850.00 for pest control services, with no income for two weeks. God proved to me that I did not need to worry about my daily needs, I know that he will make a way out of no way. It seems like magic, the key is for us is to not doubt and to know that God will work things out in our best interest in His own way and time.

AWAKENING TO OUR DIVINE SELF
The truth taught by the mystics of all ages is: Life is lived from the inside to the outside. This means that the whole universe is concentrated at the point where you are. You are the universe expressing as itself in a smaller dimension. You are its living enterprise. It forever stands behind you with its full resources. However, the fullness of this support comes through you and not to you. The most profound knowledge that you can attain is that your whole existence flows from a universal process, which is always from within to without.

There is a widespread and deep-seated belief that we are in competition with people and in conflict with the world around us. Our fears, resentment, anger, and grief come because we feel that the instability of life in the world is a threat to our existence in it. Jesus gave us the answer when he stated that, "The kingdom of God is Within You".

This mystical kingdom is the focus of the universe and the flow of the universe within each of us. This is made unmistakably clear as Jesus said, "It is your Father's good pleasure to give you the kingdom." There is a longing at the heart of the universe to flow forth into and to perfect all that has been created. This is the basis of all healing, success and overcoming. The kingdom within is the realm of all-potentiality, all-substance, all-life, all-love and all-peace. Jesus said: "Do not be anxious about your life, but seek first the Kingdom and all things shall be yours." In other words, when we step into our Divine Being and Divine knowing, we are connected to God, the Universe. We are in the Divine flow and will receive all that we desire or need. Our goal is to be in the flow of life and flow with the universe.

There are two ways to use our minds. The first use of the mind is to identify and name things in our environment. A second way to use our mind is to think about things, conceptualize and to understand.

The mind is capable of being used in a third way: It can be directed inward toward its source. It is this movement that is responsible for those moments of unparalleled happiness, when all worry and fear slips away, and we are into total contentment. The technique of Inner Focus and Inner Knowing embraces this third movement of the mind, where you maintain attitudes of positive thoughts, and affirmations. This positive inner awareness can be used throughout the day, with the eyes open or closed, and it will effortlessly draw the mind away from chaotic thought into the endless peace and stillness of its source.

WHAT IS THE PURPOSE OF LIFE?

I want to jolt you out of your usual thinking and have you look at your life, your experiences, your reason for being on the planet and Angels in a new light. Have you ever thought or wondered why we are here, what are we to do and how can you be a part of God's Divine plan? Our greatest dilemma is that we are both human and Divine. We have a human outer body and an inner spiritual body.

THE EFFECT OF CHOICE ON FEELINGS AND ATTITUDE

It is in the category of moral choices, that we are given free rein. Sometimes our feeling and emotional states can be so powerful, that we get locked into our bodily sensations and reactions and lose sight of our spiritual nature. Our thought, feelings, and emotional state determine what we do and how we react. We can experience many feeling states — Rage, compassion, murder or Love. The brain does not know the difference between these, it only knows what it sees and what it feels. Love can be connected with pain, abuse, violence, or peace. Love can be connected to anything. Everything we do, remember or say is colored by the experiences we have. If you get angry, frustrated, or suffer on a daily basis, this emotional state will keep re-firing the cells in your brain, which will create a pattern for this in your brain and your body. All emotion is holographic. This is the basis of addictions. Addiction is a cascade of feelings. It is what's inside of us, our spiritual nature that is most important to our Divine purpose for being on the planet.

Most of us do not see ourselves as Divine; however, we are both human and divine. Our body is a unique work of art. The body has many physical outlets (sex drive/reproduction, hormonal thyroid adrenal gland etc.) emotions (passion, emotional highs and lows). It has so many fascinating inner workings that it is easy for us to become hypnotized with the workings of our physical body and lose sight that we are Divine beings as well. We are a high energy, sex-driven society. We tend to worship the physical body through our sports endeavors; however, we can use our relationship with others as a tool to help us connect to our Divine inner self. We can learn how to connect with others on an emotional and spiritual level through our relationships. And our relationships can help us connect with our Divinity.

Relationships are a way to open our heart to unconditional love. Sexual energy is a powerful intoxicating energetic state. If this energy is centered entirely on the heart, one can obtain access to higher love dimensions. If this energy is directed toward the heart chakra, we can experience our Divine self in an entirely different way. Our relationships with others can be non sexual as well as sexual. If our sexual energy is not connected with the heart it can cause confusion, loneliness, agitation, a feeling of searching in the dark and we can lose ourselves into our humanness and lose sight of our Divine self. Some people are in a stage of development in which they can connect their sexual energy with their higher energy centers without a physical partner. These people can be loving partners with mankind and nature. The loving connection between man and woman on an energetic level can bring about a perfect merge that results in an awakening of their Divine energy field. The opening of the crown Christ chakra can be achieved through any relationship that involves loving compassion and non-judgement. Loving relationships result in the possibility of heart connections without our ego, and this can be a way to experience unconditional love, which leads to a higher state of consciousness; and awakening of our Christ-consciousness. All interpersonal relationship, such as a friendship, a parent-child relationship, as well as friendly relationships with animals and nature in general can lead to an awakening of the Christ-consciousness if our intention is Divine love.

I realize more everyday that I am here for a Divine purpose, that I do not have to compare my life or myself with anyone and that I am here to complete my individual contract with God. That I am Earth Angel, a Seer and Seek, which is what I suspected, long ago. This frightened me a long time ago as a child and young adult, because I had no one to explain to me, that I was here for a bigger purpose. Today I have the ability like Jesus to cast out demons from children and adults. I do not have a clue as to how I do it, I just know it happens. I realize now that I am a seer, I can see into the past and into the future through the Divine spirit of God working through me. I am a Divine Being, an Earth Angel.

Also, I realize now that I have been thinking and acting Small most of my life, and that God wanted to use me in a larger way for a larger purpose, to travel around the world, to cast out Demons and heal the planet. I realize my life is not my own and that I need to let go my notion of having a normal life, doing what I want, but to answer the Calling for me to travel (which I do not like) and let God use me to heal the planet. I am sure I agreed to this assignment before I came to earth, but do not remember.

I believe we are both Human and Divine and that we are here on a mission to carry out God's plan for humanity. That as we awaken, and gain more spiritual insight, God reveals more of himself to us and the role we are to play in helping him heal the planet. We are all here for different reasons. Some of us are here to heal the environment, some like Oprah is here to teach us about kindness and compassion, yet others like Elyse Hope Killoran and myself are here to help us let go our fears around Money (security). I am also here as a Healer, to help heal the planet and awaken people to their Divine self, that we are children of God, that we are Divine Angelic Beings, here to earn our wings through our service to humanity and return home to God.

I realize now that I used to separate myself from God when I was in my 20s in college. I valued my intellect, I was smart and had a good memory. I took pride in my intellect and gave God no credit. I thought I had gotten my intellect from my dad. and I was proud. Even though I was a Christian, I saw no connection between God and my intellect. I thought God was only in charge of my spirit and soul. I have a different awareness, now that I am in my 50s and going through menopause; my memory has been severally affected. It is not as fire crackling sharp as it used to be, so I am thankful whenever I remember someone's name. I never had a problem remembering people's name, now I get frustrated when the name does not readily come to me. Sometimes, I remember the person's name ten minutes after they have walked away. I felt embarrassed to say this to the person when they were in my presence that I did not remember their name.

Now I am thankful to God when I do remember their names. I am no longer arrogant and separated from God. I am connected to God and thankful, God did not give up on me and still loved me in spite of my lack of acknowledgement of Him. God's love for us is always unconditional and forgiving. Maturation, sometimes referred to as aging teaches us a lot of things. I can understand now why we need to age and grow older. We become wiser and more appreciative of life, living and our bodily functions. I do not take anything for granted any more. I wish I had perfect hearing like I did fifteen years ago. However, I have bought a hearing aid which is too loud, so I am learning to lip read, and turn the music up louder.

THE LONG JOURNEY HOME
In many ways the longest journey we will ever have is from the head to the heart. Our mind always wants to be right, wants to justify, or judge someone or something. Our heart, however, has no need to be right or to justify. The heart simply wants to love and understand. When things are the bleakest, know there is still hope

By quieting our minds and going deep within our hearts, we are able to allow both truths to coexist in the spaciousness of a bigger mind and heart. Our grief becomes just grief. The stretched heart hurts but can hold it all. We learn to see the uniqueness of every person and situation and the interconnectedness that binds each of us to everything.

If I have learned anything in relating to others is that each one of us must be treated with meticulous individuality. The more we stereotype people and warehouse them into groups such as (prisoners, mentally ill, condemned), the less we can see who they are and be of help to humanity.

If we refuse to label others, stereotype, categorize or prejudge people, we will see the process of loving caring take place. We are then able for the acorn inside us to become a great oak.

As we learn to forgive, we live from the spirit of our heart instead of from a spirit of judgment. There is no defense against a loving heart response. When two hearts meet and come to an agreement, healing occurs. As our level of love and understanding grows and deepens, our relationships with others are able to grow and expand in a profound and intimate way. Intimacy is an invitation to look inside the heart of another without judgment and see the inner soul of the person.

This journey from the head to heart is the one true path that can change our lives. We are an empty form, without concern, love and compassion for ourselves and others. Love is the core of us. Like the sun, love can be hidden by clouds of fear, negativity and limited beliefs; however, its fire is never put out. It is a part of the game of life. In her poem Cherie Carter Scott gives us ten rules for living.

If Life is a Game,
These are the Ten Rules for Being Human
1. You will receive a body.
2. You will be presented with lessons.
3. There are no mistakes, only lessons.
4. A lesson is repeated until learned.
5. Learning does not end.
6. "There" is no better place than here.
7. Others are only mirrors of you.
8. What you make of your life is up to you.
9. Your answers lie inside of you.
10. You will forget all of this at birth.

CHERIE CARTER-SCOTT, PH.D.

THE SECRET TO LETTING GO OUR ATTACHMENTS
Often when we are trying to manifest something we really want, we may want it so much we become attached to it. Then we try out all sorts of strategies, techniques and exercises to get "unattached", as our desired outcome seems to get further and further away. When you become overly attached to any thought, feeling or idea, your body becomes rigid and you feel that this thing *must* manifest for you to be happy or find peace with life. The truth is that joy, peace and contentment is always available to us, it is just that we are unaware of how to achieve it. When we are in the moment, we are too close to a situation to see it clearly. All situations change with time. Being attached to any desire can causes it to manifest slowly. The more you can gently hold your desire, yet be firm in your belief, it will manifest into your life more quickly.

The great secret to letting go our attachment and manifesting our desired outcome, is to consciously let in the feeling that your desired outcome is already taking place. Remember that your main task is to trust, let go, and know that God (the Universe) is working in your favor. We have to listen attentively to every thought and feeling that occurs to us.

When you make this leap of trust your body will immediately relax, since it believes on some level, it has already manifested its desire. The difference between visualizing your outcome manifesting for you effortlessly, and trying to visualize it happening to you, is defined by how immersed you are in the *feelings* of trusting the Universe. Often when you visualize something you want to manifest, your body gets tight, you worry and feel frustrated. The secret to this happening is to remain present to the feeling that your desire *is* being manifested, the Universe is listening; then practice allowing *in* feelings of relief and trust to know the satisfaction of having achieved your desired outcome.

How to Let Go Your Attachment to Things and People

Often when we are trying to manifest something we really want, we may want it so much that we become fearful it will not happen. Buddha once said, "Attachment will lead to suffering." Jesus said "Thou shall have no other God's before me;" meaning we should not make God's of people or things. Everything is temporal and dies as you too will die one day. When you become overly attached to any thought, feeling or idea, your body becomes rigid and you feel that this thing *must* manifest in order for you to be happy, or find peace with life. The truth is that joy, peace and relaxation is available to you now. All situation change with the passage of time. Being attached to *any* desire blocks out its life force and energy. The gentler you can lovingly hold your desire in a relaxed state of mind, void of fear, the sooner it will manifest.

Develop the belief that what you want, wants you. Learn to trust and know that we live in an orderly Universe. All thoughts are acted on depending on your ability to let go and let the Universe/God take over. God is attentive to every thought and feeling you have. He or the Universe repays you with a positive outcome.

When you make this leap of trust a sense of peacefulness will come over you because you are no longer pushing or forcing, but allowing for a natural evolution of what you want to come forth. Notice how relaxed your body feels when you let go your fears about not reaching your goals. This poem on our greatest fear *says it better*.

Our Deepest Fear

Our deepest fear is not that we are inadequate.
Our deepest fear is that we are powerful beyond measure.
It is our light, not our darkness, that most frightens us.

We ask our selves, who am I to be brilliant, gorgeous, talented and fabulous?
Actually, who are you not to be?
You are a child of God.
Your playing small doesn't serve the world.
There's nothing enlightened about shrinking so that other people won't feel insecure around you.
We are born to make manifest the glory of God that is within us.
It is not just in some of us, it's in everyone.
As we let our own light shine, we unconsciously give other people permission to do the same.
And as we are liberated from our own fear, our presence automatically liberates others.

— Marianne Williamson

On Responsibility

Senior citizens are constantly criticized for every conceivable deficiency of the modern world, real or imaginary. We take responsibility for all we have done and do not blame others. However, upon reflection, we would like to point out that it was not the senior citizens who took the melody out of music.

— Author Unknown

Shakespeare, Leonardo DaVinci, Benjamin Franklin and Abraham Lincoln never saw a movie, heard a radio, or looked at television. They had "loneliness" and knew what to do with it. They were not afraid of being lonely because they knew that was when the creative mood in them would work.

— Carl Sandburg

The cure for loneliness, strange as it may seem, is not in more active involvement in the world but in seeking active un-foldment from within our essential isolated self.
— Eric Butterworth

Don't try to flee from your loneliness, you'll only find it in the end. Just get acquainted with yourself, and you will gain an understanding friend.
— Author Unknown

Chapter 2

Our Angelic Quest

Today, we see an awareness and increased interest in angels throughout the world. Are you aware of the many roles angels can play in your life? Angels are all around you. They can offer you hope, guidance, solace from grief and comfort. Angels will show you how to recognize their presence and invoke the warmth, encouragement, and spiritual guidance they offer.

When I was age five, my mom sat my sister and me down in the living room in front of a large picture of an Angel, following a little boy and girl across a broken bridge. She told us that we always had an angel who watched over us wherever we went, to keep us safe from harm. I remember feeling very good about this. It gave me a sense of peace and reassurance that even if my mother was not around I was divinely protected at all times. It helped me to be unafraid, wherever I went from that time on. I always had a feeling of peace, that my Guardian Angel would never let any harm come to me.

When I left home at age 17 to go to nursing school in Chicago, I was unafraid, because I knew my Guardian Angel would follow me everywhere I went and protect me, from harm and danger. Even though the picture of the Angel and two little children remained on the wall in my mom's home in Florida, I was certain that my Angel had followed me to Chicago. That picture of the angel became imprinted in my memory bank. I later moved from Chicago to San Diego California. I looked everywhere for twenty years trying to find a picture like the one my mom had in her living room. I finally found one, she was black rather than white and I loved her just as much. When it comes to Angels, I love them regardless of their skin color. I am now aware that Angels are of every race and nationality

About three years ago, I became aware that I had more than one Angel and they had names. I was introduced to the Archangels: Michael, Gabriel, Raphael and Uriel. I could not see them however, but they spoke to me in my ear, the way God spoke to Moses. At first I did not know how to connect with my Angels. Later I discovered that the Archangel Raphael is represented by the color green. Looking back, I realize that my favorite color changed from blue to green in 1993. I could not understand why I was compelled to wear something green every day. My last name was Greene; I drove a green car and I had a green mailbox in front of my house. I was in need of healing, so God sent Raphael to help me. Raphael means "God Cures".

God gave us Raphael to provide us with healing. He charged Raphael with the responsibility of healing the Earth and its people. It is Raphael's job to cure us, to purify our blood stream, to repair the organs of our bodies so that we can eliminate stress and suffering from our life on earth every day. We have been given free will, so we must give ourselves over to Raphael so that he can perform these functions of healing for us. We must allow him to come into our lives to cleanse us of the pain and suffering of everyday life on Earth.

Learn to listen to your body, and take care of it. Nurture it as needed, and allow God to provide you the energy to overcome whatever aliments you may experience. This is Raphael's message to you.

Raphael is the Guardian Angel of Healing — persons in the

healing profession such as Doctors, Nurses and Counselors under Rapheal's healing energies. Remember, Archangel Raphael's name means "God Heals". Archangel Raphael is the Archangel that supervises healers and healing for all the earth's population. When you need healing it is wise to call upon Archangel Raphael. You can ask Raphael for help when you are in any kind of pain, whether it is physical, emotional, romantic, intellectual, or spiritual. He will inspire you with ideas and thoughts giving you the right information to help in the healing process. When asked for healing assistance, Raphael surrounds and nurtures people with the emerald green light of his halo. Green is the color of healing. Many clairvoyant people say they see emerald green sparkles when Raphael is around. Raphael is always associated with healers and healing.

I started working as a nurses aide in high school, and went on to graduate as a Registered Nurse from Provident Hospital School of Nursing in Chicago. I am certain Raphael has been with me through out my nursing career. I later worked as a School Nurse, then as a School counselor. Today I have a private practice as a Licensed Marriage, Family Child Therapist. Because of the helping career paths I chose, the Archangel Raphael has been with me most of my life.

I was unaware of the help and influence of Angels in my life until the year 2000, when I started counseling exclusively with children and they kept reporting to me that they saw Angels during my counseling and visualization sessions with them. I did not know what to make of this, I was intrigued by all the things they revealed to me about Angels. They saw Doves, golden stair cases, heaven, Jesus and many of the prophets in the Bible such as Matthew, Paul, Mark, James, Noah, Jonah, Ruth, Mary, mother of Jesus and others biblical characters. I could never see what they saw. I am Clairaudient, I hear messages in my ear the way Moses heard the voice of God, however you may hear the message in your mind. Some people are Clairsentient. Clairsentience is associated with recurring physical and emotional feelings which indicate Divine guidance. Claircognizance is when thought and ideas come to you, often they are answers to your prayers. We have to learn how to be still inside our body to hear the voice of God, or messages from our Angels. Meditation helps me to quite the chatter of noise in my head so that I can hear the still small voice of God and my Angels and the messages they give me. It is now easy for me to hear the messages from the Angels given to the children I counsel. I now incorporate Angels as part of my treatment protocol when I counsel Attention Deficit Hyperactive children. I encourage them to ask their Angels for help when they are unable to focus and pay attention in the classroom.

I now know my purpose for why I came to the planet. It is to help spread light and love in the world through the help of my Angels. I also have been given the gift of healing. I have great healing energy that flows from my hand. I was afraid of this when God gave it to me in 1990. I lost the gift due to my fear of having it. Today I have a better understanding of spiritual gifts from the Holy Spirit, so I am thankful and most appreciative to God for this gift. I realize now that when I told God, twenty years ago that He could use my hands, eyes, and every part of my body to bring about His Kingdom on earth, He heard me and did that. I am no longer afraid; I just realize more than ever that my body does not belong to me. I now allow myself to be used by God to bring about His Kingdom on Earth. I go where I am told to go, I do what I am prompted to do and I say what I am told to say to the appropriate person. I do not always understand it. I just know that I have to be obedient to the will of God. My life works when I listen to the voice of God and do His will.

What is your purpose for living? Did you ever wonder why God created you, What are you here to do, who are you supposed to help? I believe we are Angelic Earthly beings, who are trying to earn our wings so that we can find our way back home to God. We are Angelic beings, Earth Angels. God has revealed to me that He want me to commission people to become Earth Angels to help heal the planet of the dark, negative satanic energy vibrations among our youth and people today.

Some questions you may be thinking are: Who is an Earth Angel or who can be an Earth Angel? It all seem mysterious at first, however you have what it takes to be an Earth Angel.

We go in and out of our body each day, into a dream like state sometimes referred to as soul travel. When we are in these states of mind we come in contact with unholy, unhealthy beings, which can invade our energy field and wreck havoc in our physical, spiritual body. This is why we need to watch the thoughts we think and cleanse our energy field through prayer, meditation, relaxation techniques, and energy cleansing through Reiki.

To better connect with your angels you need to have your body free of mind altering drugs and have clear boundaries about what you will not do to pollute or harm your body. Watch the thoughts you entertain. Negative thoughts allow negative energy to enter into your body. We have to create a positive environment and loving aura around ourselves before our Angels can come into our body. Right brain activities like visualization, prayer and meditation helps us to connect with our Angels more readily and helps us to see and experience them better.

I now use Angels in my counseling of ADHD children. I tell the Attention Deficit Hyperactive children to ask their angels to help them with self-control and help them to focus when they are in school. I teach the children to touch their forehead, breathe in deeply three times as a reminder for them to be present in the classroom, to be focused, feel their body movement and get grounded to what is happening to them in their physical environment with the teacher and their classmates.

THE DIFFERENCE BETWEEN ANGELS AND SPIRIT GUIDES

Spirit Guides have lived before in a body. Angels have never lived in a human body; they have no knowledge of what it is like to have emotions and feelings of being in love, having a family, having children or working on a job. The exception to Angels never living before according to Doreen Virtue, Ph.D. is Archangel Metatrone, he was Enoch in the holy bible and Sandaphone was Elijah, both were elevated by God to the status of an Archangel due to their Divine work with God. During one of my meditations I was told that "Mary" the mother of Jesus is also an Angel. Whenever I do Angel Readings with children they always see and say mother "Mary" is one of their Angels. The children always see doves, golden staircases and Angels flying around in the room when I do my counseling sessions with them.

I call on the Angels to help me with my complex and difficult cases. The younger the child the easier it is for them to see Angels. I try the Angels first before I recommend medication. I am convinced that much of the Hyperactivity in children is due to many parents use of television as a baby sitter. Today, the brain of children is continually bombarded with magnetic rays from the television. They do not have the gift of day dreaming and being alone in the silence as I did as a child. This bombardment of their nervous system occurs before birth with mothers working long hours at work, being stressed from driving in commuter traffic, worrying about paying bills, drinking coffee, drinking alcohol, taking drugs and not taking time to relax, or unwind with a walk by the ocean, or walk among the trees to recharge the cells of their body. We have created the fast food baby chain today. Children come into the world today with an overly charged nervous system and are hyperactive.

The Angels are always ready to help you; however they will never intervene unless invited. Ask your Angels often for their help. Ask them for their names. Ask how many Angels do you have? Ask them what you need to know each day. Always say, I Surrender to the will of God. Your Angels are waiting to help you; however, you have to ask for their help. God has given you free will to choose "yes" or "no" to any condition or situation that confronts you in life. All Angels are under the authority of Jesus; each is associated with a color and has distinct energy vibration. Everyone has at least twelve specialty Angels. I will list them separately, so when you commune with your Angels through meditation, you can write down their name, color and any other information revealed to you.

1. Guardian Angel
2. Life Angel
3. Purpose Angel
4. Destiny Angel
5. Power/Strength Angel
6. Relationship Angel
7. Success/Career Angel
8. Finance/Good Fortune Angel
9. Health Angel
10. Spiritual Angel
11. Protector Angel
12. Home/Fertility Angel.

You have other powerful Angels who are waiting to assist you, other than the ones I mentioned. They are the Angels of:

1. **Vision**: The Angel of Vision will help you get a clear view of what you want in life, where you need to go in life and provide a vision of what is for your highest good.
2. **Wisdom**: Wisdom can help you bring your intention of perfection into fruition. This Angel can help you with the right action to take.
3. **Purity**: keep the channels clear, helps with the flow of abundance, this Angel can help on clarity of purpose and trust; help you handle fear and stay on track with your goals. Also acquaints us with the Divine.
4. **Strength**: helps you with the powerful truths: You are a powerful being, you deserve what you desire in life, and it is never too late to start. Gives you the strength and stamina to do what you need.
5. **Love**: Sometime you may judge an act, or action as unloving or unkind, you may need love to show up in a particular form for you to learn a lesson or appreciate the person who creates the challenge or brings you the message. A diamond needs a lot of friction and polishing to shine its greatest.
6. **Peace**: You will need to learn patience to become a peaceful person. If you are quarrelsome and argumentative with everyone, you cannot be in two states at the same time. You will be either a peace maker or a peace breaker. You will either spread peace or you will create a negative warring space. The Angel of Peace can help.
7. **Victory**: We can only have victory after we have gone through some of the above emotional states. The Angel of Victory helps us create endings and closure to events so we can feel victorious.

When we have gone through the fires of chaos and confusion,

we learn to have a clear vision of what we want to do and be. We learn to ask our Angel of Wisdom for guidance. The Angel of Purity can help you with clarity of purpose and help you stay on track with your goals. The Angel of Strength can provide you with the courage you need to accept that you are a powerful being. The Angel of Love will help you see obstacles and challenges as vehicles of love, and the Angel of Peace can help you stand strong as you grow through the trials and challenges presented you to achieve Victory over your lower nature to arrive at your Divine Self.

You have the power of the spoken word. You can command any condition or situation to depart from you. If you faith is weak, then you can always call upon your Angels to help you. And you can always speak the name of Jesus to remove any demonic energies or entities that may be residing in your body that create confusion or havoc. When you surrender your life to God all of your daily needs, money, health, and relationships will be perfect. If you are having a problem with someone, you can speak to the Angel of the other person and ask for help in bringing forth better communication between the two of you.

You can also ask your Money Angel for help to remove any blockages to your money flow. I have given my life over to God to do as He will; I tell myself and others that I am employed by God, now God always provides all the money I need. When you become employed by God, your life is no longer your own, you have to go where God tells you to go and do what God tells you to do. I resisted this at first, because I like to be in control of everything, then I realized I had very little control over the things that happened to me in life. so I decided to Let Go and Let God Have His Way in my body, mind and affairs. My life is more peaceful and serene and I always have money in my possession.

In the book, "Your Daily Angel," there are many other

Angels listed: Angel Damaliah help with Spiritual Protection, Angel Mankel with Relationships; Angel Mehiel-Psychic Perception, and Angel Nemamiah-Prosperity; and Angel Mumiah helps with Miracles.

Archangels are a higher order of Angels. There are 12 Archangels: four of them are in the Bible

1. Michael — Protection
2. Gabriel — Angel of Communication
3. Raphael — Healer
4. Uriel — Angel of Light

In the book *Commune with the Angels,* Jane Howard lists the three Hierarchies and the Nine Choirs of Angels According to Dionysus. At the highest level are:

1. The Throne of God Angels (energy of constancy)
2. The Supreme Hierarchy, in terms of their vibration, consists of the Seraphim, Cherubim and Thrones
3. The Middle Hierarchy consists of the Dominions, Virtues and Powers Angels
4. The Lower Hierarchy consist of the Principalities, Archangels, Angels which I will list below with their function in which they serve and help us.
5. Humankind are divine beings with angelic traits.

Angels serve in many roles. The Angel Vehuiah helps with envisioning new beginnings. Angel Jeliel is associated with fertility; she helps you maximize your creative senses and assists with growth. The Angel of Triumph, Sitael, encourages you to expand your horizons. Angel Elemiah helps with Travel and Adventure. The Angel of Enrichment delights in seeing you blossom like the flowers around you. The Angel Haziel, helps with Domestic Harmony, The Angel of Purification, Aladiah will help you if you are about to start a new diet and want to change your habits to become a healthier you. Whatever Angel you ask for help they all want you to love yourself.

I Love Myself

Deep at the center of my being, there is an infinite well of love. I now allow this love to flow to the surface.

It fills my heart, my body, my mind, my consciousness, my very being, and radiates out from me in all directions and returns to me multiplied.

The more love I use and give, the more I have to give. The supply is endless. This use of love makes me feel good. It is an expression of my inner joy.

I love myself, therefore, I take loving care of my body. I lovingly feed it nourishing foods and beverages.

I lovingly groom it and dress it, and my body responds lovingly to me with vibrant health and energy.

I love myself, therefore I lovingly provide a comfortable home for myself that fills all my needs and is a pleasure to be in.

I fill the rooms with the vibrations of love so that all who enter, me included, will feel loved and be nourished by it.

I love myself, therefore, I work at a job that I truly enjoy, one that uses my creative talents and abilities. I work with and for people I love and who love me, and I am earning a good income.

I love myself, therefore, I behave and think in a loving way to all people for I know that which I give out returns to me multiplied. I attract only loving people in my world for they are a mirror of who I am.

I love myself, therefore, I forgive, release the past and all past experiences, and I am set free.

I love myself, therefore, **I love *in the now***. I experience each moment as good and know that my future is bright, joyous, and secure for I am a beloved child of the universe and the universe lovingly takes care of me now and forever. And so it is.

— ADAPTED BY IDA GREENE

HOW TO STEP INTO YOUR ANGELIC DIVINE SELF

Angels can work miracles for you if you let them. It is easy to call upon them and find the Health, Wealth and Happiness you want. Have you ever wondered: Who are my Angels? What are their roles in the ranks of Heaven? How can I get in touch with them? How can I communicate with my Angels, anytime, anywhere? What can my Angels do for me? How can they change my life?

- Angelic help is available; all you have to do is ask your Angels for better health, true love, peace of mind, even the funds to settle your debts and gain some security, your Angels can help you make your fondest wishes come true. That blessed day when you entered the world, an Angel was with and watching over you. This Angel who is still beside you today, is ready to assist you, all you have to do is ask for your Guardian Angel.
- Your Guardian Angel has been your companion throughout your entire life. He/she is with you right now, waiting to give you its divine help so that you can claim the success and rewards you were born to enjoy. Have you ever really heard your Angel's message? Do you know his or her name, how you can reach your Angel/s and accept their offer to transform your life?

- Legend tells us that the seven Principal Angels have special powers over different areas of human life. The powers of your personal Angel are reflected in your particular gifts and talents, and in the challenges you face during your life time. Many people believe Angels have a mission: to shield us from harm and guide us toward a happier, more fulfilling life. Even researchers at the Harvard Divinity School and Boston College, feel that Angels move between levels of the universe to deliver messages to us from Heaven; messages that are intended to lead humanity to a more perfect existence, and help us to reach our highest potential.

This is wonderful news because it means that besides having Jesus, if you are a Christian, who lend help and support when you face any challenge in life, you also have Angels. Angels are messenger from God. Even if you think you've never felt the healing presence of your Angel, it's likely they have already tried to touch and comfort you.

Perhaps you once narrowly escaped being hurt in an accident, or recovered miraculously from a bad illness, or felt a strange sense of comfort during one of the hardest times of your life. **That might well have been the hand of your Angel reaching out to you**. It is important that you know which Angel to call upon, depending on what it is you need. You'll read stories of people just like yourself whose lives have been transformed through the touch of their Angels. **Get to know your personal Angels to let them bring more joy into your life.**

Be kind to everyone; because everyone is creating a space for you to be transformed; even those you think are obstructing you, or those whom you think are enemies. Your friends, your enemies, good people, bad people, favorable circumstances, unfavorable circumstances; all are creating the context in which you can be transformed to become a Divine being, so be grateful to all people, situations and events. Be grateful to those who have helped, to those who have hindered you, to those who have been indifferent. A diamond needs a lot of polishing to shine its greatest. Be grateful to all, because all together they are creating the context where Christ is born within you, so you can take on the habits, attitude and mind set of the Divine. *There is a time for everything,* (ECCLESIASTES 3:1-8.)

A Time for Everything

There is a time for everything, and
a season for every activity under the sun:
a time to be born and a time to die,
a time to plant and a time to uproot,
a time to kill and a time to heal,
a time to tear down and a time to build,
a time to weep and a time to laugh,
a time to mourn and a time to dance,
a time to scatter stoned and a time to gather them,
a time to embrace and a time to refrain,
a time to search and a time to give up,
a time to keep and a time to give up,
a time to keep and a time to throw away,
a time to tear and a time to mend,
a time to be silent and a time to speak,
a time to love and a time to hate,
a time for war and a time for peace.

Commitment

Until one is committed there is hesitancy,
The chance to draw back is Always ineffectiveness.
Concerning all acts of initiative

And creating there is one elementary truth,
The ignorance of which kills countless ideas
And splendid plans;
The moment one definitely commits oneself,
All sorts of things begin to happen that would
 never otherwise would have occurred
A whole stream of events issues from
The committed decision,
Raising in one's favor all matter of incidents,
meetings and material assistance,
Which no person could have dreamed
Would come their way.
Whatever you can do, or dream you can begin.
Boldness has genius, power and magic in it.
Begin it now...
— GOETHE

Ten Ways to Bring Spirit into Your Relationships
AVALON DE WITT

Whether you want to deepen your marriage, attract a mate, or just get along better with your boss, it always helps when you bring Spirit into your relationships. Many times we get caught up in "taking care of business" in relationships and we go through the motions, forgetting all about Spirit. When you bring Spirit to your relationships, you are drawing from a power that is infinite. How can we do that more? Here are some starters:

1. Listen

Really listen. Don't try to "do active listening," or any other listening technique. When you're concentrating on a technique, you're not listening. Just take in what the other person has to say. Receive the meaning of the message, without immediately jumping to respond to the message. Listening helps you connect with people. Spirit loves to show up when people are connecting.

2. Practice Non-judgment
You never know how something might serve the ultimate good in the long run. It is not up to us to decide that the other person is right or wrong, good or bad. This does not mean you cannot assess things in your relationships. You can assess whether someone is being sincere, honest, or trustworthy. We just don't have to assign a value judgment to that, by saying it is good or bad. It just Is. And what you make of it - is up to you.

3. Seek to Understand the Other
Don't worry about being misunderstood. When you drop your concern about that, and get curious about understanding the other person, two things happen. First, you stop stressing yourself about what others think of you. Second, you show the other person that they are important to you. When the other person sees that they are genuinely important to you, they will generally return the feeling. Not to mention, being able to understand another person feels good, and feeling good always brings Spirit to relationships.

4. Be Honest
If someone likes you for something that you do, then it's not you that they like. Be who you are. Most people will respect you for your honesty, even if they don't agree with you. But don't go along with others just to please them, if it doesn't please you too. People will sense your discomfort and you may not know why, which will create tension in the relationship where it's not necessary. Be true to yourself by speaking up and telling the truth about who you are and what you desire. "If you're not

being true to yourself, you're not being true to anyone else."

5. Eat Together
You've got to break bread together. And it can't be just a hamburger in the car on the way to a show. There is no substitute for sitting down and sharing a meal with a person. Animals will not eat when they are threatened. When you eat with someone, you are showing them that you trust them. And when two people trust each other, THERE is Spirit.

6. Stop Analyzing the Relationship
Stop analyzing, stop worrying about the future of your relationship and just BE in the relationship. Enjoy the relationship here and now. The here and now — is your bridge to the future. If you are spending your today's worrying about your tomorrows, you're not here, in today, doing what it takes to build something that can endure.

7. Say Thank You
The more you are thankful, the more you will have to be thankful for. And of course, people usually like being thanked. Saying thank you is like returning what's been given to you, with interest, except it doesn't cost you anything. Most of the time, thanking someone will make you feel just as good as the other person feels hearing it, sometimes even better.

8. Look to See What You Can Learn
When we are open to learning, we are expanding. When we are expanding, we are growing. When we are growing, that's the work of Spirit. There is always something more for us to learn. When we stop learning, we stop growing, and when we're not growing, we're dying. Learn, and live!

9. Be Selfish

I'm talking Selfish, NOT selfish. Self with a big "S," not a small one. (What you are doing in the relationship needs to be more important to you than what the other person is doing in the relationship, if you want Spirit to show up.) You can't control the other person. You can't always know what another person's intentions are. But you can control yourself, and you can know your own intentions. When you concentrate on your own desires, intentions and actions, rather than those of the other person, you are taking responsibility for your part in the relationship. No one else can do that for you. Be responsible for getting your needs met.

10. Know that You Are Beautiful

The spirit inside of you came from The Divine Light. If you are alive, you have light inside of you, and that light is beautiful. When you see the beauty in yourself, it's easier to see it in others. Enjoy the beauty that is in you. Admire it. Let it make you smile, the way the beauty of a child or a sunset makes you smile. Your sense of beauty will become contagious.

Remember that the purpose of relationships is to help you with your spiritual growth. Every interaction you have with another person is an opportunity to become more of who you truly are. Spirit is the breath of life in relationships. Without it, we fall short of connecting with others. Bring more of Spirit to your relationships and watch how much easier it is to get along, and to find fulfillment in all your interactions.

Connect with Your Angels

Use your Inner Angel for immediate, easy and effortless success. Your Angels will never intrude into your life. They have to be invited by you to give you messages from God and help you with your daily affairs. We have been given the power to say "yes" or "no" to the circumstances and situations that confront us each day. You have the power of the spoken word. You can speak to any condition in your life to neutralize or empower the situation. All angels are under the rulership of Jesus, so you have the ability to receive healing energies that can transform you and your life.

Chapter 3

How To Connect With Your Guardian Angel

DEVELOP YOUR SELF-ESTEEM TO CONNECT WITH YOUR ANGELS

Your Magnificent Self

The essence of you is divine. It is pure Spirit. You are God's child, therefore you one with the body and mind of God. God is: Joy, Peace, Love, Compassion, Understanding, Perfection, Abundance, Prosperity, Health, Wealth, Contentment, Harmonious Relationships, Tranquility, Intelligence, Wisdom, All Knowing, and Pure Spirit that never dies. You are not separate from God and God is not separate from you. Since our mind is one with the mind of God, God communicates with us through our thoughts-our ideas, intuition, inspirations, and aspirations.

It is the Spirit of God working in and through you, when you get an idea to do good for others, to serve mankind, to perform an act of kindness, lend a helping hand to those less fortunate than you, feed the hungry, help the homeless, say hello to a stranger, smile when someone gives you a frown, a cold shoulder or give you the finger, because you inadvertently moved your car over in front of them too close. You respond with love to their anger, or when someone gossips about you and you do not take the offense personally, it is the Spirit of God pouring out through you.

If you could see yourself as God sees you, you would never doubt yourself, feel inadequate, feel broke, sad, lonely, poor, disappointed, limited, inferior, or worry about anything. When you keep your thought uplifted on God and his goodness, you will see miracles take place in you life on a daily basis. Keep you thoughts focused on all that is: Good, wholesome, pure, joyous, loving, kind, generous, giving, opulent, inspiring, abundant, and peaceful, for this is the Essence of God and God is the Essence of you.

You are perfect just as you are, never compare yourself to another person and never wish you were someone else. You are you and that is enough. God made each person different from the other. We are his flower garden. You have a fragrance like no other human being. You have a soul and spirit like no other person. Let your music sing, tell your story of how God brought you through a difficult challenge. Your Father/Mother/God loves you very much. You are his precious child and He will never leave you or abandon you. You are Beautiful, You are Powerful, and you can be All Knowing when you put on the mind of the Christ. Believe in yourself, never doubt yourself, and pray for wisdom when in doubt. Your prayer can be as simple as — God, please help me or show me the way. Remember, who you are. You are Divine — You are the Essence of God and that is more than enough.

Osho says, "You are carrying a masterpiece hidden within you, but you are standing in the way. Just move aside, then the masterpiece will be revealed. Everyone is a masterpiece, because God never gives birth to anything less than that. Everyone carries a masterpiece within them hidden for many lives, not knowing who they are and trying on the surface to become someone. Drop the idea of becoming someone, you are already a masterpiece. You cannot be improved. You have only to come to it, know it, and realize it. God himself has created you; you cannot be improved."

I like the notion that we cannot be improved and is perfect as we are. Our society has bought into the notion, that we are flawed from birth. I believe in self-improvement to enhance who we are, I feel we are each unique. We are a flower waiting to burst forth into the full bloom of our magnificence and ecstacy.

THE BENEFITS OF LEARNING HOW TO CONNECT WITH YOUR ANGELS.

You can learn:
1. How to have a simple, two-way communication with your own personal team of spiritual helpers, so that you can ask them as many questions as you want throughout the day
2. How to use your intuition to communicate with yourself, other people and your angels through the four spiritual gifts of Prophecy, Clairvoyance, Clairaudience and Healing.
3. How many spiritual guides you brought with you and why you chose each one, so that you can pinpoint the exact area of your life where each one is here to help you.
4. What part, the exact percentage (i.e. 100%? 90%? 80% etc.) you are directing your personal energy in a positive way — and how much of your energy you are wasting on indecision and negative thoughts (this information comes directly from your own personal angels. Most of the time you are listening to your spiritual helpers on a daily basis. Are you doing this 100%? 80% 20?.

Discover how to listen more intently to the 80 to 90 hunches, visions, ideas and feelings, that your angels give you daily.
5. The key to your personal strength or niche in life is tied to how you see yourself. Do you operate as an Administrator, Promoter, Coordinator or victim?

What is your true purpose in life?
Most people think that their life purpose is their job or profession. Nothing could be further from the truth. You have a positive spiritual message you came to share with others. It is unique to you. You have been living it your whole life…you just don't know it.

This is what you came to do. You did not come here to be a doctor, lawyer, shopkeeper or street-sweeper. You came here to live this spiritual message for yourself first, then help others to do the same thing for themselves.

To Discover Your Passion In Life,
Ask Yourself These Questions:
1. What things in life give me the greatest pleasure or satisfaction? Write about each below then put them in order of most important #1, 2.

    A. Personal: Being able to help mom or dad around the house; or help others if you are an adult:

    B. Social: Playing with friends:

    C. Spiritual: Talking to God, or your imaginary friend:

2. What things others praise or compliment you on? List below

3. Now that you have completed the activities above, <u>what thing or things</u> would you enjoy doing every day of the year, even if you were not paid money? Whatever you choose is your passion, start now and enjoy your life. *"Life Is Shorter Than You Think."*

DEVELOP YOUR SELF-WORTH TO BECOME MORE ANGELIC

What are some of the things you believe about yourself that are different from the things people say about you?

I Believe I Am	People Say I am
....	....
....	....
....	....
....	....
....	....
....	....

Things I like about myself are:

Because..........

Things I dislike about myself are:

Because........

Things I am willing to change, so I can like myself are:

My Self

I have to live with myself, and so
    I want to be fit for myself to know,
    I want to be able, as days go by, Always to look myself straight in the eye;
    I don't want to stand, with the setting sun, And hate myself for the things I've done.
    I don't want to keep on a closet shelf, A lot of secrets about myself.
    And fool myself, as I come and go, Into thinking that nobody else will know The kind of person that I really am;
    I don't want to dress up myself in sham. I want to go out with my head erect; I want to deserve all men's respect;
    But here in the struggle for fame and self, I want to be able to like myself.
    I don't want to look at myself and know, That I'm bluster and bluff and empty show,
    I never can hide myself from me; I see what others may never see;
    I know what others may never know; I never can fool myself, and so,
    Whatever happens, I want to be self-respecting and conscience free.

            — Edgar A. Guest

Discover Your Strengths to Become An Earth Angel

1. If you could do only one kind of work, what would it be?

2. Can you think of anything that sets you apart from others? e.g. friendly, considerate.

3. To discover your strengths:
   State characteristics or traits that is uniquely you.

4. To find your weaknesses:
   List faults or areas of your personality you want to improve.

5. To Enhance your self-image ask yourself, how do I see myself in relation to others, am I as good as they? If so, in what way? If not, why?

   A. Doctor

   B. Governor

   C. Waiter

   D. Trash Collector

   E. Attorney

Today

This is the beginning of a new day.
God has given me this day to use as I will.
I can waste it, or use it for good.
But what I do today is important because
I am exchanging a day of my life for it.
When tomorrow comes,
this day will be gone forever.
Leaving in its place
Something that I have traded for it.
Good and not evil,
Success and not failure,
In order that I shall not regret,
The price that I have paid for it.
— KRISTONE

AFFIRMATIONS FOR HIGH SELF-ESTEEM

Look in the Mirror Every Morning and Affirm:

1. I nurse my inner child with love in my heart. I am healed of past mistakes and errors.
2. I support my inner child. I am healed of all feelings of low self-worth
3. It is O.K. for the little child in me to succeed and be successful.
4. I accept and approve of myself. I have dominion over myself and all my affairs.
5. I am a spiritual being living a spiritual life. There is no place for doubt, anxiety, or fear.
6. Knowing that what I experience is a result of my thinking, I eliminate all negative thoughts from my mind. I accept me just as I am.
7. I accept that I live in a spiritual universe that is per-

fect, orderly, and beautiful. I see myself as a spiritual being that is perfect, orderly and beautiful.
8. I have that within me which will maintain and sustain me in all ways, for I and my Father/Mother God are one.
9. I am blessed with an abundance of all the good, life has to offer, this includes money and money substance.
10. I rejoice that I am both a child of God and a child of the earth, that all of life, both divine and human, is mine to live and to enjoy.
11. I rely on the spirit of self-reliance within me to satisfy all of my needs.
12. My way in life is made clear to me; I listen to and follow my intuition.
13. I am filled with enthusiasm; therefore I am an enthusiastic person.
14. I am worthy and deserving of all the good I can imagine and then some.
15. I love and appreciate myself.
16. I am worthy and deserving of love.
17. God loves me, I love me and that's enough.
18. I am magnificent, gorgeous, beautiful, adorable and wonderfully made by God.
19. God does not make junk, I am one of a kind, a Divine and Royal Being.
20. I accept my beautiful eyes, my luscious lips, my exquisite face, my perfectly sculptured nose, and my royal body portions.

How to Connect With Your Guardian Angel

Each of us has a Guardian Angel that watches over us to guide and protect us from harm and danger. God loves you so much that he want you to have joy and fullness of life. What is your passion, what do you want to do better, what is your motivation to be the best you can be and say Hello to Your Greatness, and Goodbye to your Smallness. Connecting with your Angel is easy. It like picking up the phone to talk with someone except this will be a mental spiritual connection to your Guardian Angel. Your Guardian Angel escorted you into the earth and will escort you out when it is time for you to make your transition back to God. We are given 70 years, three scores and ten years to refine our soul, work on our attitudes, finances, relationships, our health, our faith and work on our soul salvation of peace, harmony, integrity, honesty, commitment, being responsible, dependable, feeling worthy and deserving, unconditional love and most importantly being of service to God to help heal the planet.

Our Guardian Angels have been with us since before our birth and accompany us in every step we take in our lives. The Angels understand everything about us, they know us intimately and completely, and love us unconditionally. They increase the loving energy that we are able to feel both from our own soul and from God, the source of infinite love. They expand and amplify our ability and willingness to share this love with others. The Angels are also very practical and do their best to guide us to express our creative abilities in grounded and pragmatic ways so that we will be positive and effective as we share and work with others.

Asking an Angel for help is one of the most powerful spiritual practices you can do. We can ask the Angels for immediate help at any time and in any place.

Here are some techniques that will help you:
1. Ask for help – Our Angels offer us help twenty four hours of the day, every day of the week. The more receptive we are, the more help they can give us. If you diminish your receptivity through fear or doubt you will limit the Angels ability to help you. Create your own invocations, or prayers, that specifically call for the help you need. Realize that when you call upon an Angel, what really happens is that you open yourself to greater receptivity to their assistance.

    When asking for help, it's important to realize yourself as fully worthy of Angelic assistance. Angels work with everyone regardless of personal histories and beliefs. Angels are infinite and omnipresent — your request does not diminish them in anyway nor does it affect their ability to help anyone else at the same time. They exist beyond our experience of time and space and respond to everyone with complete unconditional love.
2) Connect with your inner divine child as you call upon the Angels and ask for help. Your inner divine child is whole, innocent and true and recognizes Angels as trustworthy gifts of the Creator. Accepting this belief will help create openness, receptivity, excitement, eagerness and wonder as you prepare to receive the gift your Angels have prepared for you.
3) Hand everything over to the Angels when you ask for their help: every issue, problem, worry and fear as well as every good intention and positive outcome you imagine as the result of your request from them. Release all expectations of how your request will be answered.
4) Express Appreciation and Gratitude — Find and express genuine appreciation and gratitude for things

exactly as they are. If you are struggling with this, ask the Angels to help you find the love that is present in whatever difficulty you are facing. Have patience with this and let go of any expectation of how this love may be revealed to you.

5) Know that it is done – Every request is answered and help is always given. If you fear that your request will not be answered, then also ask for help in understanding and letting go fear. Trust that you will see the love in every answered prayer. You are known completely and loved unconditionally by the Angels and nothing that can serve you is ever withheld from you.

6) *Act quickly on the guidance you receive from your Angel.* Accept the information and act upon it immediately. Angelic help is infinite and unlimited — you can not use it up or run out of it. You cannot ask for "too much" and the Angels are joyous and happy to give to you without limit. The faster you act, the faster you receive more assistance.

7) Celebrate yourself exactly as you are in the moment. Leave any critical judgments or negative feelings about yourself, your life, or others in the hands of the Angels for healing. Even if it is just for a few moments, let go of everything that is not of love for yourself and everything around you. In this moment of surrender, much more can done for you by the Angels than you can accomplish on your own. Thank yourself and the Angels for deepening the relationship between you and them.

The fastest way to connect with your Angel/s is to start meditating from five to fifteen minutes a day. The ultimate goal is to meditate twenty minutes, two times a day. These are the steps to meditation, if you want, try it now. Sit in a straight back chair, in loosely fitted clothing, with your feet flat on the floor. Gently close your eyes while you breathe in deeply and exhale at the count of three. Go into meditation with the intention of wanting to see and wanting to make a connection with your Guardian Angel. Picture a white light all around you and focus on your breathing. If you get distracted easily put on some relaxing music. You may fall asleep when you first start to meditate however, be patient with yourself and continue with your counting and breathing until you have a break through. If you persist and are unsuccessful, you can call me for a phone consultation to help you deepen your meditative experience.

I am trained in Reiki energy balancing and I am a healer. I have been anointed with the holy spirit of God and Divine energy flow through my body. You have the same ability, it just takes praying, trusting, talking to God and asking for this Gift. I did not ask for the gift, however, I told God he could use my body to bring about His kingdom on earth and he did. You can call me for an Angel consultation by phone for a nominal fee. We can address any topics you like or we can go into prayer and meditation to introduce you to your twelve Angels. Call Angel Ida at 619-262-9951. I also have books, tapes and CDs to help deepen you meditative state and open up your awareness to the Divinity inside you. Go to www.idagreene.com or we can consult for a fee by e-mail idagreene@idagreene.com.

Some thoughts to ponder during your meditative experience with your angel/s: Are Angels a higher order of beings than humans?

Scriptural Reference about Angels

"What is man that you are mindful of him, You made him a little lower than the heavenly beings and crowned him with glory and honor." PSALM 8:4-5, NIV.

Scriptural References to Angels

Angels can appear in the form of ordinary people. *"Do not forget to entertain strangers, for by so doing some people have entertained angels without knowing it."* HEBREWS 13:2, NIV

Who is the leader in charge of the angels? *"And now Christ is in heaven, sitting in the place of honor next to God the Father, with all the angels and powers of heaven bowing before Him and obeying Him."* I PETER 3:22, TLB

Angels are special Guardians. *"Beware that you don't look down upon a single one of these little children. For I tell you that in heaven their Angels have constant access to My Father."* MATTHEW 18:10, TLB

Angels provide protection. *"For He will command His angels concerning you to guard you in all your ways; they will lift you up in their hands, so that you will not strike your foot against a stone."* PSALM 91:10-11, NIV.

Angels rescue us from danger. *"For the angel of the Lord guards and rescues all who reverence Him."* PSALM 34:7, TLB.

Angels carry out God's orders. *"Bless the Lord, you mighty angels of His who carry out His orders, listening for each of His commands. Yes, bless the Lord, you armies of His angels who serve Him constantly."* PSALM 103:20-21, TLB.

Angels carry God's messages. *"An angel of the Lord appeared to them, and the glory of the Lord shone around them, and the angel said to them, 'Do not be afraid. I bring you good news of great joy that will be for all the people, for unto you is born this day, in the city of David, a Savior, who is Christ the Lord, and this shall be a sign unto you, you shall find the babe, lying in a manger, wrapped in swaddling clothes."* Luke 2:9-10, NIV.

The Tibetan Book of Living and Dying
1. I walk down the street, There is a deep hole
   in the sidewalk
   I fall in. I am lost… hopeless.
   It isn't my fault. It takes forever to find a way out.
2. I walk down the same street.
   There is a deep whole in the sidewalk.
   I pretend I don't see it.
   I fall in again.
   I can't believe I'm in the same place.
   But it isn't my fault.
   It still takes a long time to get out.
3. I walk down the same street.
   There is a deep hole in the sidewalk.
   I see it is there.
   I still fall into it…it's a habit.
   My eyes are open now.
   I know where I am.
   It is my fault.
   I get out immediately.
4. I walk down the same street.
   There is a deep hole in the sidewalk
   I walk around it.
5. I walk down another street.
   Poem from *The Tibetan Book of Living and Dying*

The man who goes alone can start today, but he who travels with another must wait till that other is ready.
— HENRY DAVID THOREAU

If a man does not keep pace with his companions perhaps it is because he hears a different drummer. Let him step to the music he hears, however measured and far away. — AUTHOR UNKNOWN

Twenty years from now you will be more disappointed by the things you didn't do than by the ones you did do.
So throw off the bowlines.
Sail away from the safe harbor.
Catch the trade winds in your sails.
Explore. Dream. Discover. — MARK TWAIN

A thousand mile journey begins with one step. — LAU TZU

Be as the still mountain
Move like the great river. — AUTHOR UNKNOWN

An optimist is a person who sees a green light everywhere, while a pessimist sees only the red stoplight. The truly wise person is color-blind. — ALBERT SCHWEITZER

Until he extends his circle of compassion to include all living things, man will not himself find peace.
— AUTHOR UNKNOWN

Example is not the main thing in influencing others. It is the only thing. — AUTHOR UNKNOWN

We can easily forgive a child who is afraid of the dark; the real tragedy of life is when men are afraid of the light. — PLATO (427-347 BC)

It is one of the commonest mistakes to consider that the limit of our power of perception is also the limit of all there is to perceive. — C.W. LEADBEATER

If you were going to die soon and had only one phone call you could make, whom would you call and what would you say? And why are you waiting?
— STEPHEN LEVINE

Aim at heaven and you get earth thrown in. Aim at earth and you get neither. — C.S. LEWIS

Good timber does not grow with ease; the stronger the wind, the stronger the trees. — J WILLARD MARRIOTT

Security is mostly superstition. It does not exist in nature, nor do the children of men as a whole experience it. Avoiding danger is no safer in the long run than outright exposure. Life is either a daring experience, or nothing. To keep our faces toward change and behave like free spirits in the presence of fate is strength undefeatable. — HELEN KELLER (FROM "LET US HAVE FAITH")

There is nothing more tragic than to find an individual bogged down in the length of life, devoid of breadth.
— MARTIN LUTHER KING, JR.

People are like stained-glass windows, they sparkle and shine when the sun is out, but when the darkness sets in, and their true beauty is revealed only if there is a light from within. — ELISABETH KUBLER-ROSS

A human being is part of a whole, called by us the Universe, a part limited in time and space. He experiences himself, his thoughts and feelings, as something separated from the rest – a kind of optical delusion of his consciousness. This delusion is a kind of prison for us, restricting us to our personal desires and to affection for a few persons nearest us. Our task must be to free ourselves from this prison by widening our circles of compassion to embrace all living creatures and the whole of nature in its beauty. — AUTHOR UNKNOWN

To understand the heart and mind of a person, do not look at what he has already achieved, but at what he aspires to achieve. — AUTHOR UNKNOWN

In three words I can sum up everything I've learned about life: it goes on. — AUTHOR UNKNOWN

You are an Angel,
as well as a struggling human,
but you are not a struggling Angel. — AUTHOR UNKNOWN.

Is truth so particular, that there is only one gate to heaven? There are no gates. Heaven is inside you.
You are not even the gatekeeper. — ROBERT FROST

Finish every day and be done with it. You have done what you could.
Some blunders and absurdities no doubt crept in, forget them as soon as you can. Tomorrow is a new day; you can begin it well and serenely. — AUTHOR UNKNOWN

Chapter 4

Angels Among Us, Earth Angels What Is An Earth Angel?

The time has come for those with a higher vision of what our world can be to realize that something extraordinary is actually *happening* on the planet. That in spite of the appearance of insanity — which is simply the death throes of the old paradigm — A Higher Consciousness *is* arising *in* millions of people around the world whose hearts and *minds* are open. Open to an expanded, enlightened vision of what it means to be a human. You are free to dedicate time, energy and resources as a true expression of Love, people who are open to experience themselves as a conscious part *of the* One.

Millions of people are participating in organized humanitarian services without an agenda. Millions more quietly do good works in their own community or beyond without the need for recognition. And many millions more with kindness in their hearts, who want to do something to alleviate the suffering of others but don't know how. The seeds of loving-kindness have never been obliterated; they have lain dormant until the moment was ripe for sprouting. They have quietly done this throughout the past decades. Now the fruit is beginning to ripen at precisely the time when the need is greatest. Now is the time to stand up and be counted. It is time for individuals who make up the multitude to know they are not alone: You are part of a great ocean of human kindness - a tidal wave of caring that is sweeping the Earth and establishing itself in every nook and cranny. There are three thing you can do every day to bring about a faster change on the planet. Begin practicing the following three steps:

1. Observe your thoughts. Think kindly of yourself and others.
2. Observe your speech. Practice kindness in your speaking in every interaction.
3. Observe your actions. Act in a way that promotes the feeling of loving-kindness within you and those around you.

These three simple steps will nourish the sprouts of loving-kindness within, and lead to the realization that *you* are actually an embodiment of the Evolution Revolution. Once *you* experience *yourself* as loving-kindness, you will recognize the loving-kindness in others. You will be led to your own role in the Evolution process and realize that you are changing the world by changing yourself. Before long we will reach critical mass and see the results of these changes everywhere. Let us start today.

I believe: We have a connection between heaven and earth through Angels.
- That there is no sex in heaven, our joy there comes from God.
- Heaven is a fourth dimension, we can see it as we evolve spiritually.
- At death the body and the soul are separated and the soul goes to heaven.
- The purpose of life is to come to the end of your life and have peace with God.

- You can find Heaven right where you are. Heaven is a state of mind.
- Everyone can be forgiven.
- The purpose of life on earth is to glorify God, and daily practice the teachings of Jesus.
- Everybody is here to help someone, no one is unimportant, we are all important.
- Believing in Heaven is important, It is our connection to God
- We are all important, no life is more important than another.
- We are all here for God's glory and satisfaction. Many of us have forgotten who we are or why we were sent. We are here to work out our soul's salvation.
- We are here to serve. Compassion can change our attitude about ourselves and others
- Love can change our heart.
- Nothing ever dies, we just change forms after death; it is life on a higher spiritual plane.
- There is nothing to fear about death, if we have a life of purpose and there is significance to our life.

I will address some of the above topics in this section. I have a better insight about the nature of life, our purpose, who we are and why we are here after reading the book and seeing the movie *The Celestine Prophesy*. The ninth insight states that everything in the universe is energy and that our conflicts, tendency to dominate and control others, even our wars is about our desire for energy. We tend to take energy away from others rather than give them energy. When we give energy to another person and they in turn give energy back to us the energy is magnified, then everything in the environment is benefited. The plants are more alive, the color hues of the plants are more vivid. In addition when we concentrate or focus on sending out positive energy into the world, our bodies will become light bearers who illuminate and enlighten the world.

I always knew our thoughts operated on the basis of a radio frequency; this is why we can tune into other people thought wave, by think about them or energetically connect with them and they will call us, or we can think their name and they will call us on the phone. When I was about six years old, I used to stare at the sky or air and see the energy waves in the environment. This is the same energy that Benjamin Franklin found in lightning and utilized it in the electric light bulb, that was used by Alexander Graham Bell in the telephone, and that is in the water dams. It is this same energy that picks up our chaotic thoughts of conflict, strife, anger, hostility, violence, war and magnifies this in the form of tornadoes, hurricanes, Tsunami, and other weather calamities.

Everything is energy and this energy can be good or bad depending upon our individual and collective energy vibrations. On the other hand, Angels, who are not human, have an energetic field that is calming, peaceful, relaxing and comforting. Maybe this is why there is an increasing interest in Angels today. I am becoming more aware of Angels now than ever before. God always speaks to me in my ear as he did to Moses in the bible. I have learned to still my mind so that I can listen and learn. It was nerve wracking at first, because I like to be in control of all aspects of my life. I finally realized that things weren't working out as I wanted, so I decided to let go and let God take over my body, mind, and affairs. This change has brought me peace and many blessings. I don't have to worry about my money or livelihood. I just tell God what I need. Usually He sends it without me asking. I am finding money all the time now. I find at least a penny everyday. All of life is about getting or having energy.

All life form need and uses some form of energy. Humans evolve from the natural man to the Divine is a progression from an animalistic nature to a refinement of the subtle energetic field of the human body and energy fields, so that it eventually is submerged with the Divine energies of God. It is at this Point that mankind will have evolved to its desired and ultimate state of being one with God. This evolvement of mankind will continue until all of mankind is energetically one with the Divine energy of God. No one knows how long it will take mankind to evolve to this state. However, it seems to me that we must move from a state of conquest and power over others to a cooperative state of trust, harmony, tranquility, peace and love of our fellowman for Christ or God to reborn in us. We must learn to give as well as receive energy. When we learn how to recycle energy, there will be no need for us to take energy from others, through power struggle — powering over others to control them, manipulation, covert or overt violence and abuse. Since everything is energy, you must not only give energy you must "allow yourself to receive, this will increase your intuition, energy level, and ability to give to others." When your energy is low or feels depleted, here are some simple steps you can take to recharge your inner battery.

How to Generate Energy Inside You
1. Get adequate sleep, 6–8 hours daily
2. Eat life giving foods such as fruits and raw vegetables
3. Exercise daily
4. Drink eight glasses of water daily, preferably alkaline or filtered water
5. Breath deeply from the abdomen often during the day

6. Minimize the intake of toxins such as coffee, refined sugar, red meat, pork, alcohol, mind altering chemicals (Crack, Cocaine, Marijuana etc.)
7. Focus on positive thoughts frequently during the day
8. Avoid people who argue, are quarrelsome or have a bad temper
9. Minimize the intake of processed foods such as French fries, pizza, and hamburgers
10. Meditate and Pray for 10–20 minutes each day

I feel God is calling upon us to change the negative energy in our youth, our environment and in ourselves. This is where my progressive interest and awareness of Angel tends to be leading me.

My God Mother who was also my cousin, died July 10, 2005, on her 93rd birthday. Since her death, I have changed my views about Angels. I realized at her funeral that she was not an ordinary person, she was an Earth Angel. She had many adopted adult children apart from her five biological children and each one felt like they were her "only" child. Even her pastor cried at her funeral because, he too was treated like a "special person", because she baked sweet potato pies just for him. I also had my own sweet potato pies, peach cobbler, macaroni and cheese, home made ice cream and Rosie B. Maull's special corn bread. I was treated like her oldest daughter because I had no relatives in San Diego.

My mom who lived in Pensacola Florida was twelve years younger than Mama Betty, her first cousin. My mother had asked mama Betty to look out for me while I lived in San Diego. Mama (cousin) Betty was 12 years older than my mom. She took care of (baby sat) my mom, and my cousin Alberta Fryson in Minters Alabama when they grew up as young children and where I was born.

My grandmother and cousin Betty's mother were sisters. Mama Betty started her Angelic nurturance at an early age. My mom who did not live an Angelic life, was an alcoholic and died at age 73. Mama Betty made up for all of my mom's shortcomings. She would come down to San Diego from Los Angeles on the Greyhound bus with her son to visit with me. She would get all of my relatives in Los Angeles in a car and bring them down to visit me in San Diego. She called me by phone monthly or I called her. She told me often how much she cared for me and told that she was only a phone call away and that I was to call her night or day if I needed something. She was my Therapist; whenever I needed to talk about something or get a second opinion, she was always available to listen to my problems. It seemed like my problems disappeared after I talked to her. I realized now that she gave me individualized attention (energy) by listening without interruption to what I was saying. This is what my dad, who died at age 60, did for me; it made me feel special and loved.

I usually went to Los Angeles every holiday to spend time with Mama Betty and the Maull clan. Mama Betty was an Earth Angel; she took her role as a nurturer and head of the family serious. I am aware now, that many of us have been called to be Earth Angel — bearers of light for truth and compassion, Divine energy and love. We have been called to reach out to the forgotten, to uplift, nurture, and heal the planet with our word of hope, joy, love and light which shine brightly from our essence. I have been called by God to be an ambassador for Christ, a barrier of Light, Love, Joy and Peace. There is too much negativity, strife, anger, hostility, and wars. We need to focus on peace, harmony, cooperation and love.

We have shifted from being a nation of peace makers to

being a nation of war monger. I feel we are in need of some Angelic help at this time in our countries and our own individual evolution. I feel it would be helpful for us to meditate on the loving vibrations of Angels, invite the Angels to enter into our personal space and body to help raise our energy vibrations to help heal our planet of fear, violence, and abuse against each other. We need the loving energy vibrations of the Angels.

We need to start acting, thinking and behaving as Angelic beings of light and love. I would like to invite you to become an Earth Angel. An Earth Angel is anyone who surrenders their life to God. They realize they are here to make a difference and they want God to use them. They see themselves as barriers of light love, peace, harmony, contentment, joy and peace. Would you like to become an Earth Angel? It is easy.

An Earth Angel is someone who commits 10, 20 or 30 acts of kindness or good deeds a day, has a loving, giving spirit and commits random acts of kindness like Flower Olivera, at a Gymnasium where I go to work out. I told her that that the locker room was dirty. I had complained to the housekeeping department, Gym supervisor and to the administrative office and got no results. Flower got a broom, dust pan, she picked up all the paper off the floor, the cleaning solution and immediately began to clean the locker room, the shower stalls and toilets seats. Flower even sprayed in the toilets, so they smelled nice. Then she said to me, I wanted you to be happy and have a good workout. I apologize for the locker room being a mess. Flower acted as an Earth Angel, she went over and beyond her job description.

An Earth Angel is anyone who performs random acts of kindness to others without reward or compensation. These are some people I feel were/are Earth Angels: Jesse Owens; Althea Gibson; Rosa Parks; All of the civil rights workers, black and white, All of the students who integrated the schools in the south like Autherine Lucy; civil rights leader, Medgar Evers, Martin Luther King Jr.; Coretta Scott King; Mother Teresa; Norman Vincent Peale, Oprah Winfrey is an Earth Angel of Giving; My God mothers — Ms. Marie McArver; Ella B Argrow; Veora Conley Brooks; Mrs. Rosa Betty Maull (mama Betty). Yvette Williams has an Angelic smile, loving spirit of acknowledgment and recognition of others. Ms. Frances Story, my Angel, serves as a volunteer with my non profit organization and does anything she can to serve the needs of the organization and the children we serve. Often when a child is very angry with me in my children's Anger Management group for my having to set limits or boundaries with them, they will snuggle next to Ms. Story for nurturance and love. I am amazed at how quickly she can calm their hot flaring tempers. She is always available and ready to assist me with any administrative task, she always say yes, just as our Angels. Do you know someone who is an Earth Angel?

An Earth Angel is anyone who performs random acts of kindness to others without reward or compensation. Their reward is seeing happiness on the faces of other people. I want to have one million people sign up on my website to become a certified Earth Angel. To become an Earth Angel, a person will need to do 10 Good Deeds a day. When you have completed your Good Deeds, send me the list with your Good deeds, and $5.00, I will mail you your certificate. You can also purchase a set of wings for a nominal fee. Please check our website for the amount. We will have monthly phone calls, prayer vigils to end violence and abuse of children, which is the mission of my non profit organization.

We will have visualization and energy work for stubborn health concerns; we will conduct Emotional Freedom energetic healing, and Divine white light healing by phone. You can sign up on my web site to be an Earth Angel. www.idagreene.com. Or send me an E-mail to: idagreene@idagreene.com My mission is to end violence and abuse of children around the world. I would like funding to set up a nationwide 800 number where any abused child in the U.S. can call in for support and help. Together we can end sexual abuse, emotional abuse, mental abuse and spiritual abuse of children. You can make a donation at www.idagreene.com Call 619-262-9951. We will meet once a month by phone to talk about how we can change the planet as Earth Angels. Love Is the Only Answer. I provide Intuitive Readings and Angel Reading by phone for a nominal fee, 619-262-9951

What lies behind us and lies before us are small matters, compared to what lies within us.
— RALPH WALDO EMERSON

A problem cannot be solved on the same level it was created.
— RALPH WALDO EMERSON

Fall in love with what you're going to do for a living. It's very important. To be able to get out of bed and do what you love for the rest of your life is beyond words. It's just great. It'll keep you around for a long time. — GEORGE BURNS

Our greatest glory is not falling, but in rising every time we fall.
— THOMAS EDISON.

THE EARTH ANGEL CONTRACT
Ten Good Deeds or Acts of Kindness

1.

2.

3.

4.

5.

6.

7.

8.

9.

10.

Bibliography

Commune With the Angels, Jane M. Howard, A.R.E. Press, Sixty-Eight & Atlantic Avenue, P.O. Box 656

Light the Fire Within You, Ida Greene, Ph.D., P.S.I. Publishers, 3639 Midway Drive, Suite B # 374, San Diego, CA 92105

Your Daily Angel Guide, International Rights, Ltd., 150 West 22nd Street, 9th Floor, New York, NY 10011

Say Goodbye to Your Smallness, Say Hello to Your Greatness, Ida Greene, Ph.D., P.S.I. Publishers, 3639 Midway Drive, Suite B # 374, San Diego, CA 92105

Testimonials

Ida communicates with a wonderful pure Being known as Isaiah. she hears easily and interprets Isaiah. He disseminates a rare radiance and purity of energy. — PAMELA M. ROMAN, MULTIDIMENSIONAL CHANNEL AND HEALER

Ida has been given the gift of spiritually touching clients and transferring an awesome purification of the client's body, mind and spirit. — QUAN AH ON

Index

Angel of –
   Enrichment, 24
   Love, 23
   Purification, 25
   Vision, 22
   Wisdom, 23
Archangel, v
   Gabriel, 16, 24
   Metatrone, 20
   Michael, 16, 24
   Raphael, 16, 17, 24
   Sandaphone, 20
   Uriel, 16, 24
Archangels, 16
Christ chakra, 7
Divine Self, 1, 4, 6, 8, 23, 26
Earth Angel, v, 7, 19, 41, 54, 59, 60, 61, 62, 63
Guardian Angel, 15, 21, 26, 34, 44, 47
Health Angel, 21
Money Angel, 23
Personal Angels, 27, 36
Purpose of Life, 5, 55, 56
Spirit Guides, 20

www.ingramcontent.com/pod-product-compliance
Lightning Source LLC
Chambersburg PA
CBHW030005050426
42451CB00006B/117